Cameron Mackintosh Presents
Boublil and Schönberg's

BIG-NOTE PIANO

Les Misérables™

A Musical by
Alain Boublil & Claude-Michel Schönberg

Lyrics by Herbert Kretzmer

ISBN 978-0-7935-2918-6

ALAIN BOUBLIL MUSIC LTD.

EXCLUSIVELY DISTRIBUTED BY

Visit Hal Leonard Online at
www.halleonard.com

Contact Us:
Hal Leonard
7777 West Bluemound Road
Milwaukee, WI 53213
Email: info@halleonard.com

In Europe contact:
Hal Leonard Europe Limited
Distribution Centre, Newmarket Road
Bury St Edmunds, Suffolk, IP33 3YB
Email: info@halleonardeurope.com

In Australia contact:
Hal Leonard Australia Pty. Ltd.
4 Lentara Court
Cheltenham, Victoria, 3192 Australia
Email: info@halleonard.com.au

Les Misérables

AT THE END OF THE DAY

Music by CLAUDE-MICHEL SCHÖNBERG
Lyrics by ALAIN BOUBLIL, JEAN-MARC NATEL
and HERBERT KRETZMER

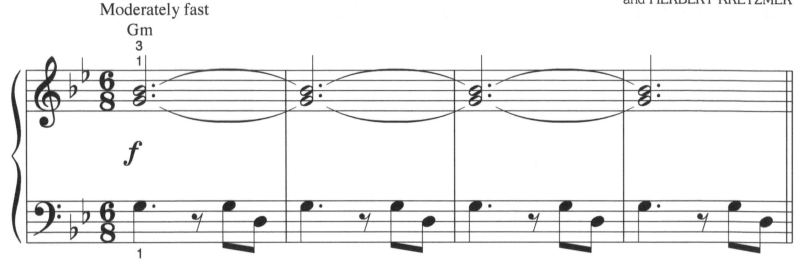

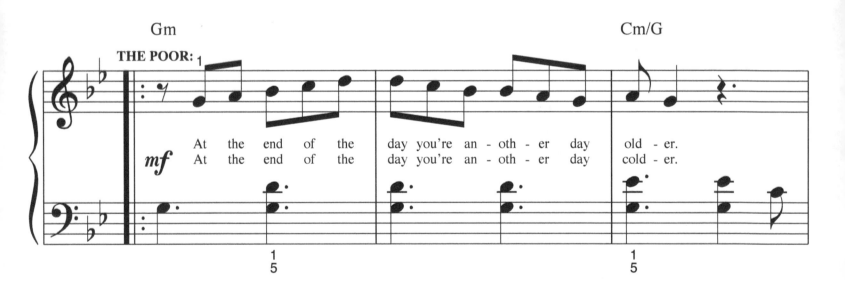

At the end of the day you're an-oth-er day old-er.
At the end of the day you're an-oth-er day cold-er.

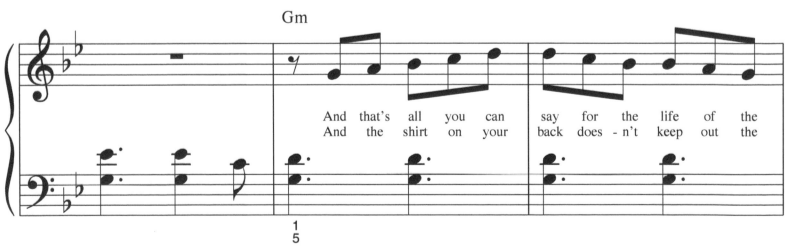

And that's all you can say for the life of the
And the shirt on your back does-n't keep out the

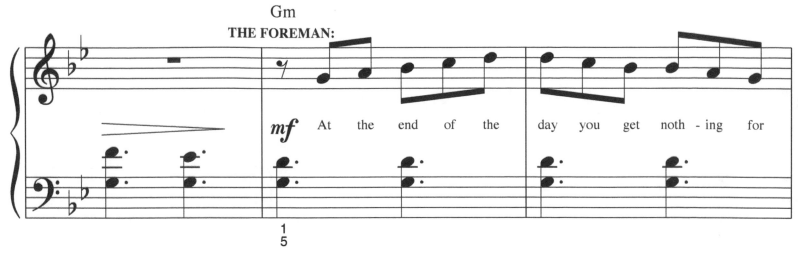

THE FOREMAN:
At the end of the day you get noth-ing for

noth-ing. Sit-ting flat on your

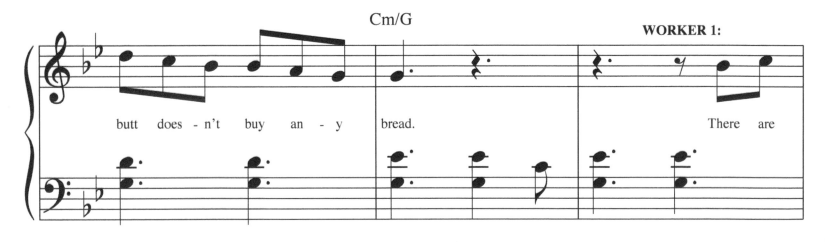

butt does-n't buy an-y bread. **WORKER 1:** There are

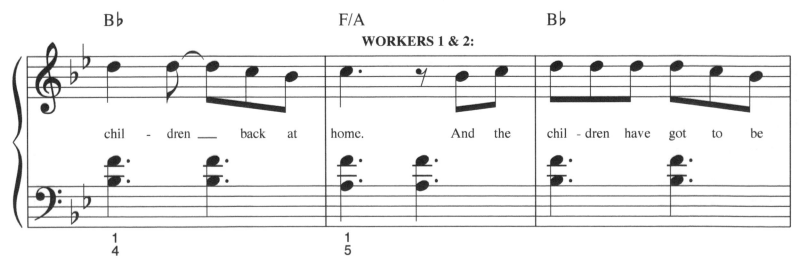

WORKERS 1 & 2:
chil-dren back at home. And the chil-dren have got to be

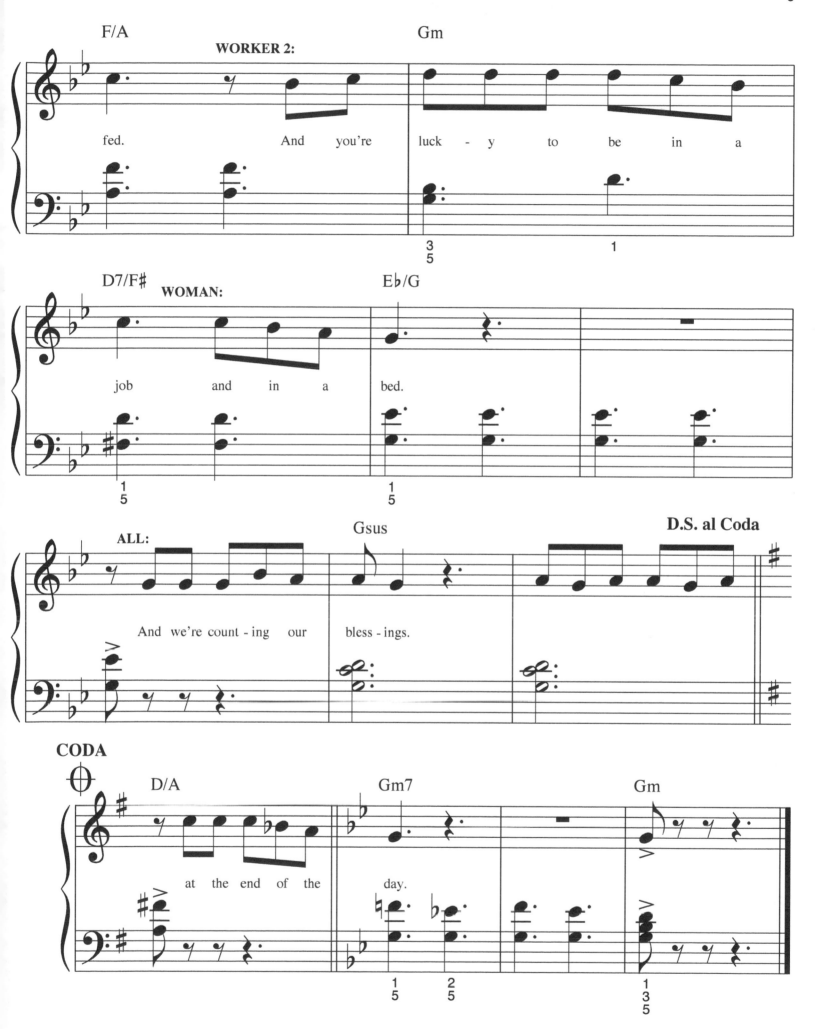

I Dreamed a Dream

Music by CLAUDE-MICHEL SCHÖNBERG
Lyrics by ALAIN BOUBLIL, JEAN-MARC NATEL
and HERBERT KRETZMER

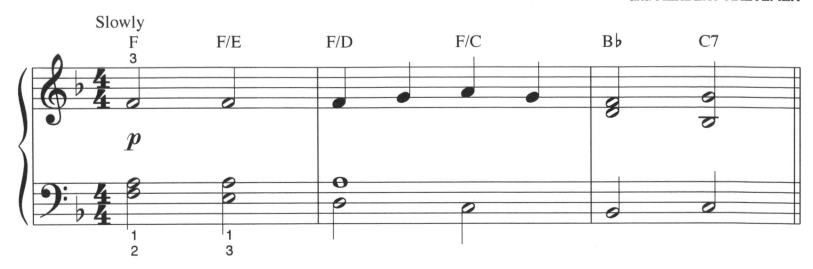

FANTINE:
I dreamed a dream in days gone by   when hope was high and life worth

liv - ing.   I dreamed that love would nev - er die.

14

WHO AM I

Music by CLAUDE-MICHEL SCHÖNBERG
Lyrics by ALAIN BOUBLIL, JEAN-MARC NATEL
and HERBERT KRETZMER

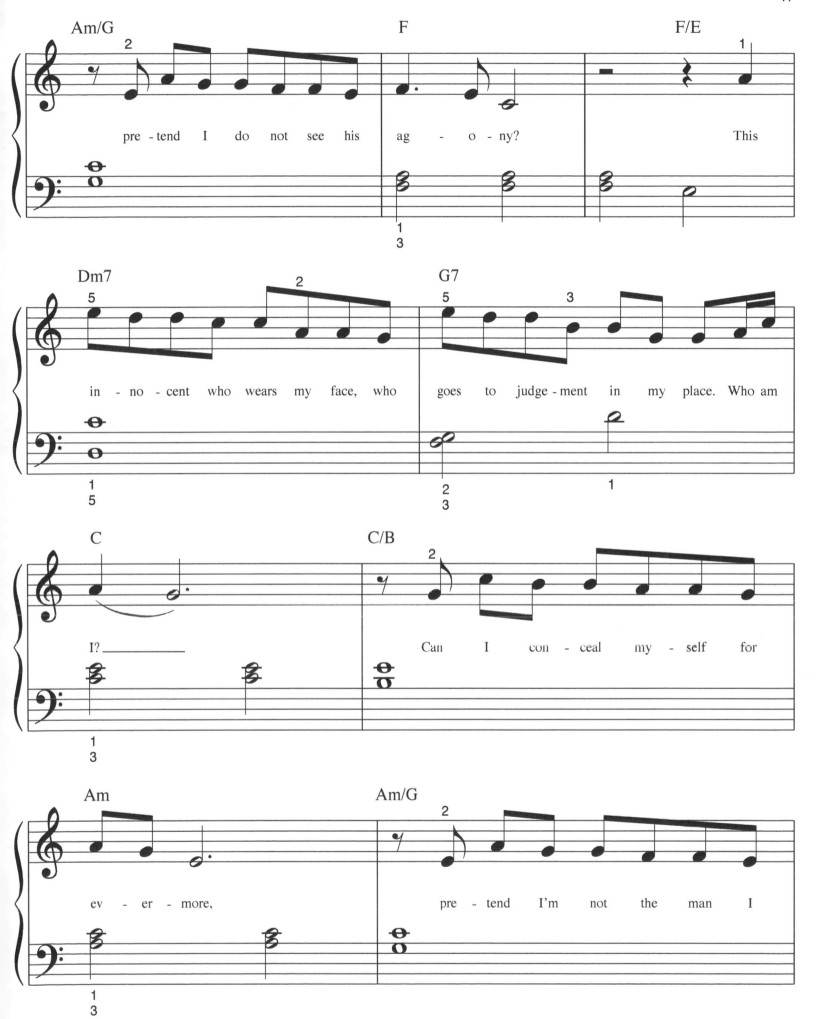

CASTLE ON A CLOUD

Music by CLAUDE-MICHEL SCHÖNBERG
Lyrics by ALAIN BOUBLIL, JEAN-MARC NATEL
and HERBERT KRETZMER

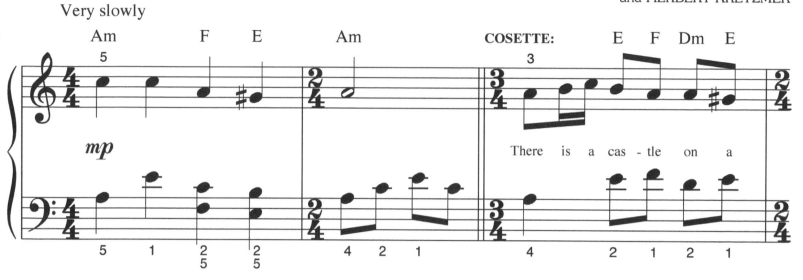

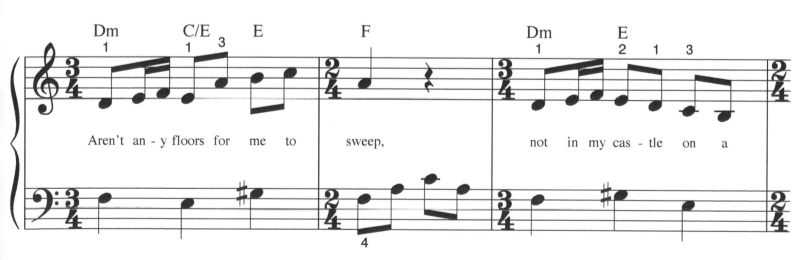

MASTER OF THE HOUSE

Music by CLAUDE-MICHEL SCHÖNBERG
Lyrics by ALAIN BOUBLIL, JEAN-MARC NATEL
and HERBERT KRETZMER

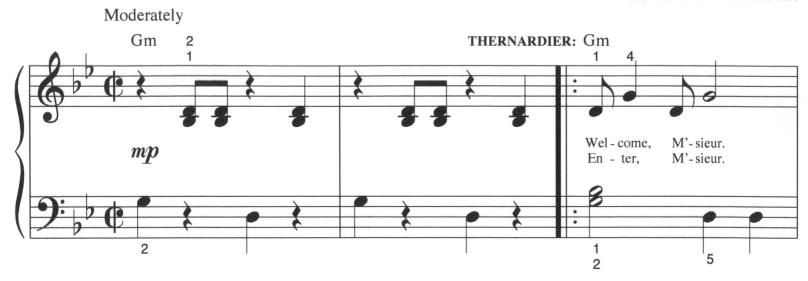

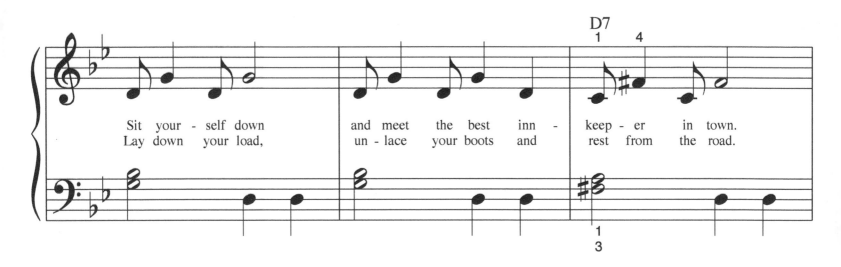

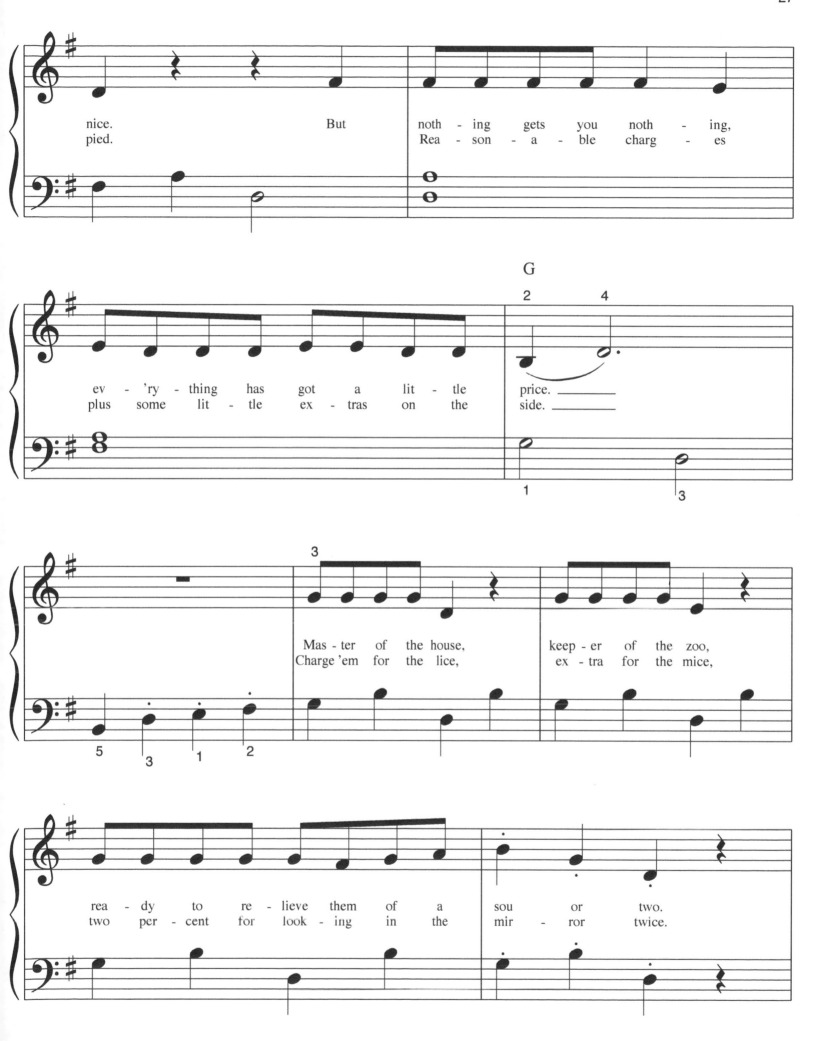

Wa - ter - ing the wine, mak - ing up the weight,
Here a lit - tle slice, there a lit - tle cut,

pick - ing up their knick - knacks when they can't see straight.
three per - cent for sleep - ing with the win - dow shut.

Ev - 'ry - bod - y loves a land - lord.
When it comes to fix - ing pri - ces,

Ev - 'ry - bod - y's bos - om
there are lots of tricks he

friend. I
knows.

do what - ev - er pleas - es,
How it all in - creas - es,

29

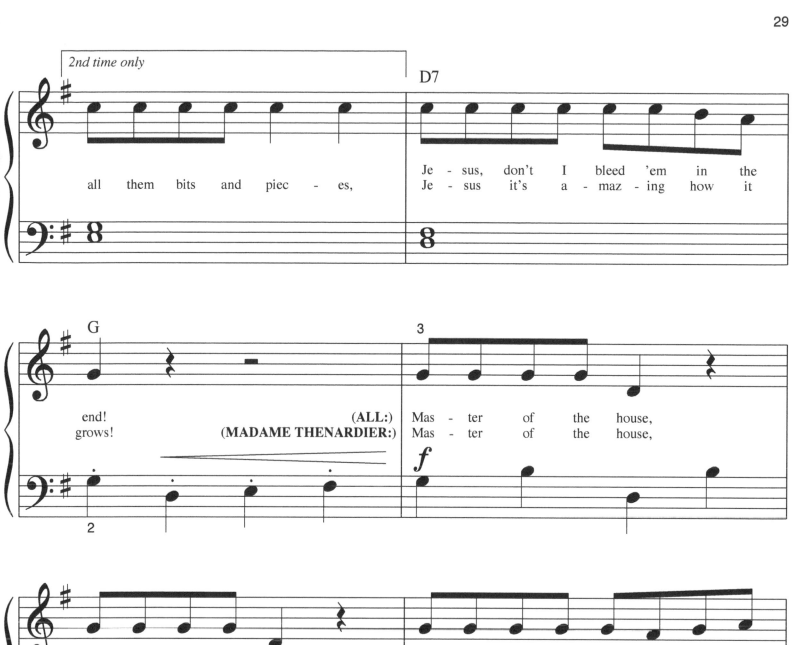

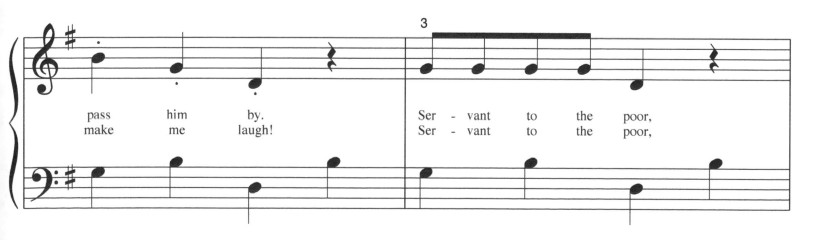

STARS

Music by CLAUDE-MICHEL SCHÖNBERG
Lyrics by HERBERT KRETZMER and ALAIN BOUBLIL

Moderately

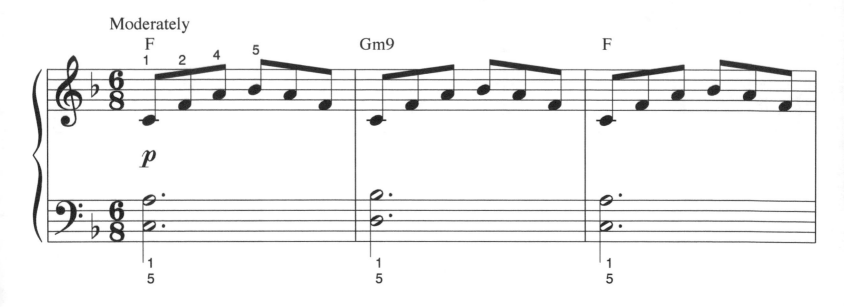

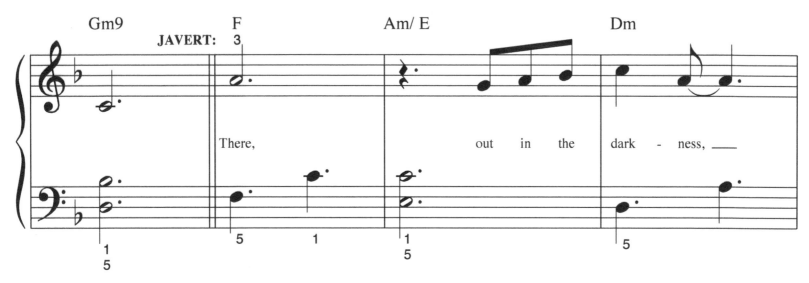

IN MY LIFE

Music by CLAUDE-MICHEL SCHÖNBERG
Lyrics by ALAIN BOUBLIL, JEAN-MARC NATEL
and HERBERT KRETZMER

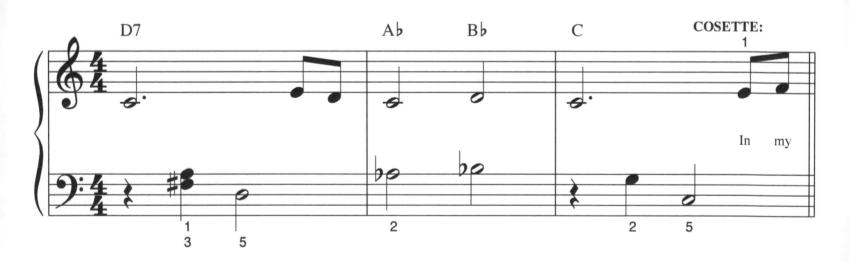

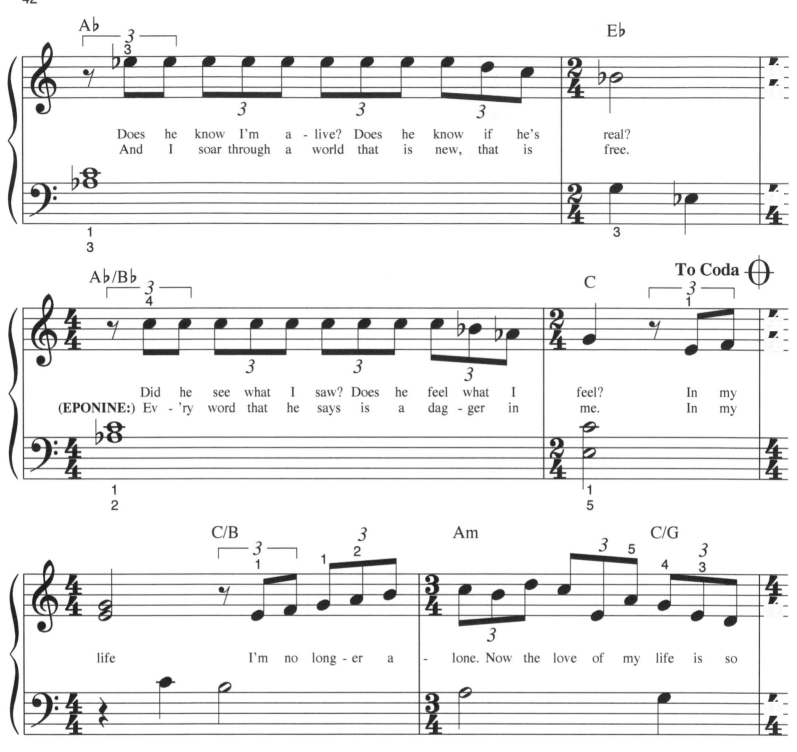

Does he know I'm a - live? Does he know if he's real?
And I soar through a world that is new, that is free.

Did he see what I saw? Does he feel what I feel? In my
(EPONINE:) Ev - 'ry word that he says is a dag - ger in me. In my

To Coda ⊕

life I'm no long - er a - lone. Now the love of my life is so

near. Find me now. Find me

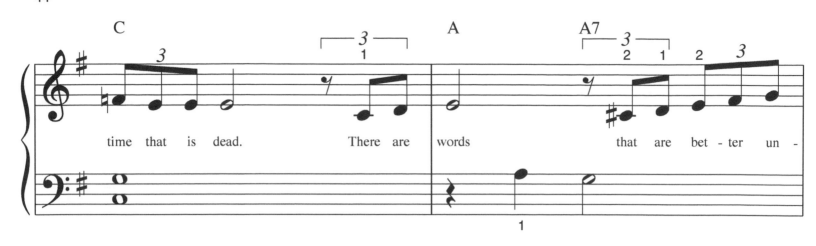

time that is dead. There are words that are bet-ter un-

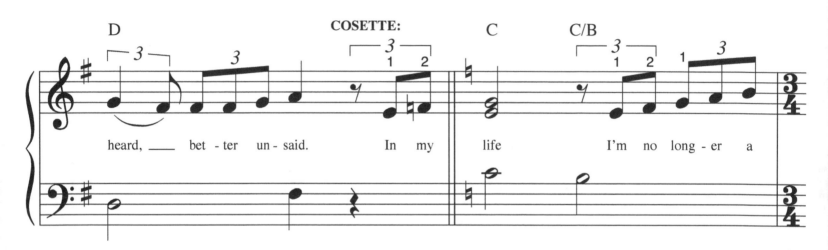

heard, ___ bet-ter un-said. In my life I'm no long-er a

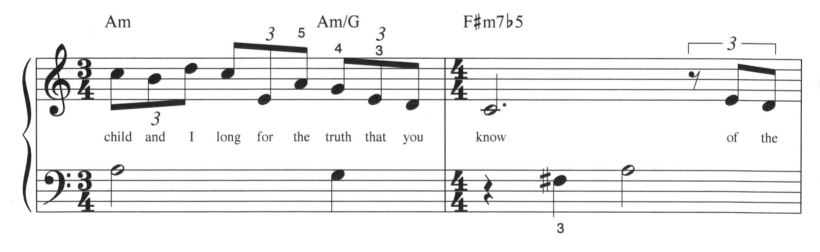

child and I long for the truth that you know of the

VALJEAN:

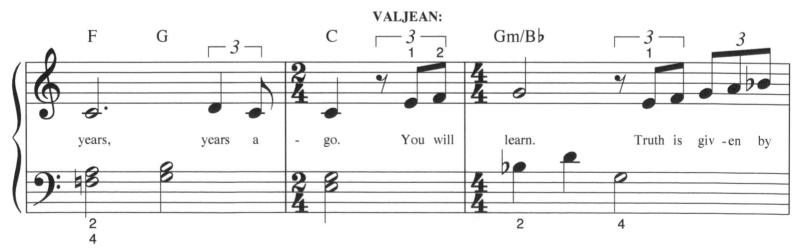

years, years a - go. You will learn. Truth is giv -en by

DO YOU HEAR THE PEOPLE SING?

Music by CLAUDE-MICHEL SCHÖNBERG
Lyrics by ALAIN BOUBLIL, JEAN-MARC NATEL
and HERBERT KRETZMER

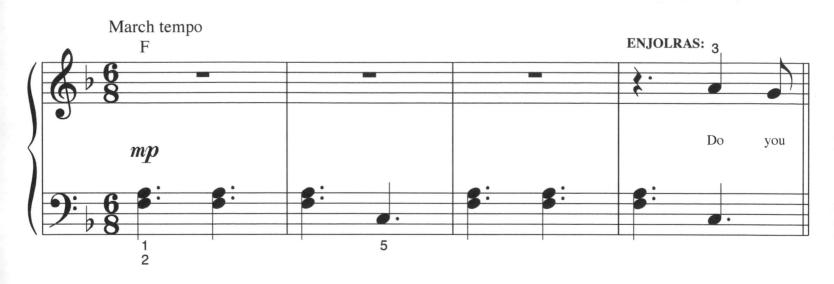

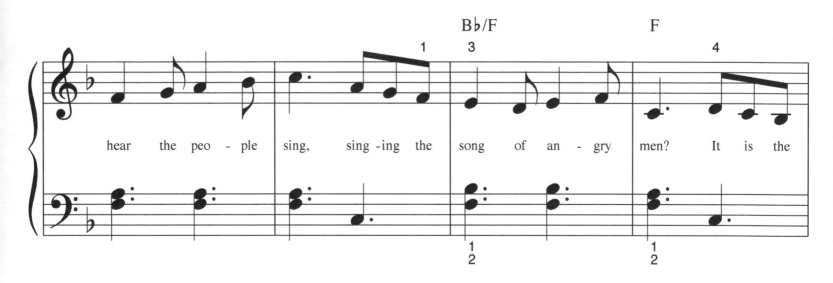

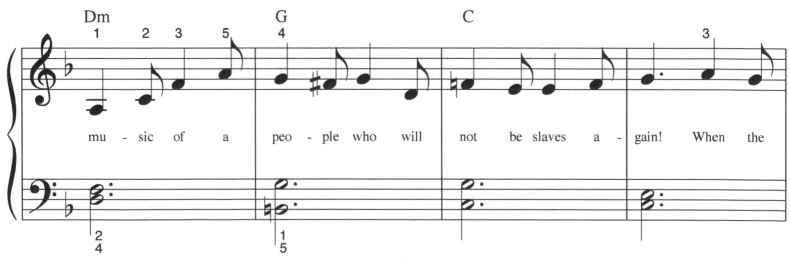

COURFEYRAC:

cade is there a world you long to see? Then
live. Will you stand up and take your chance? The

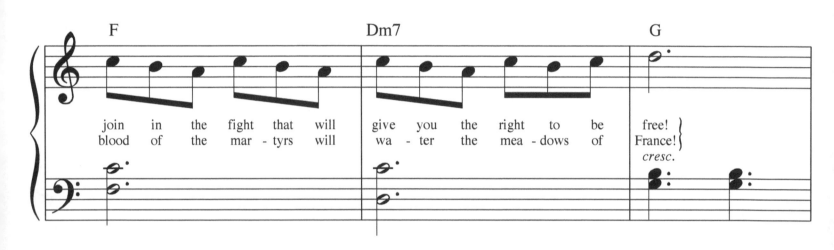

join in the fight that will give you the right to be free!
blood of the mar - tyrs will wa - ter the mea - dows of France!

cresc.

CHORUS:

Do you hear the peo - ple sing, sing - ing the

song of an - gry men? It is the mu - sic of a

A HEART FULL OF LOVE

Music by CLAUDE-MICHEL SCHÖNBERG
Lyrics by ALAIN BOUBLIL, JEAN-MARC NATEL
and HERBERT KRETZMER

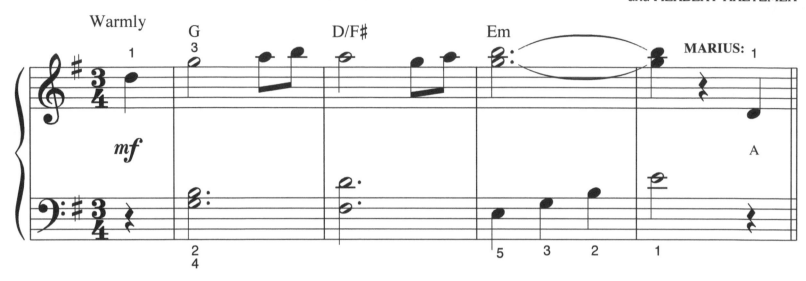

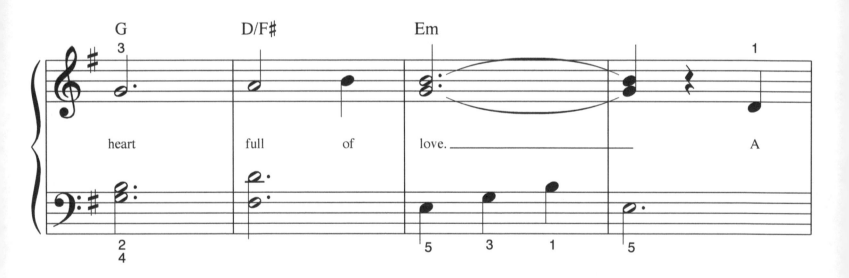

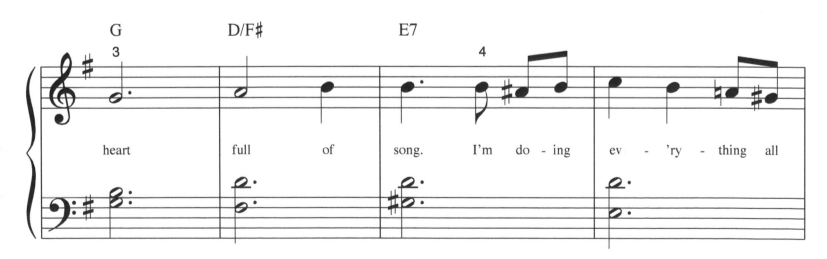

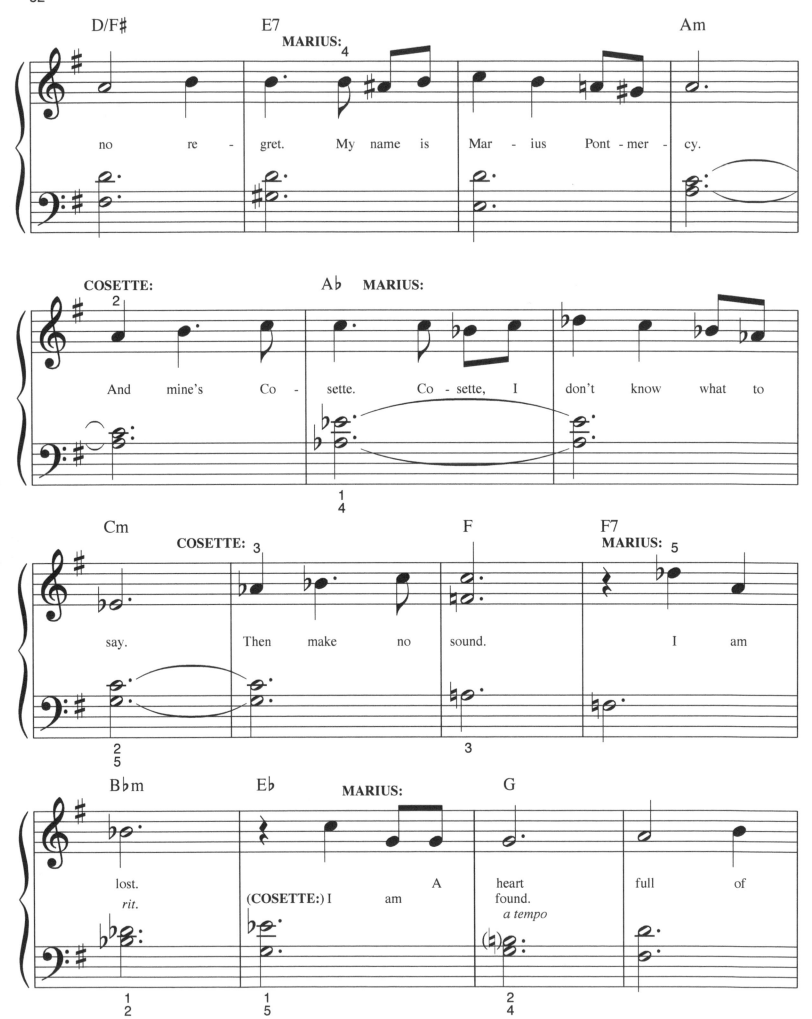

ON MY OWN

from LES MISÉRABLES

Music by CLAUDE-MICHEL SCHÖNBERG
Lyrics by ALAIN BOUBLIL, JEAN-MARC NATEL,
HERBERT KRETZMER, JOHN CAIRD
and TREVOR NUNN

Gently

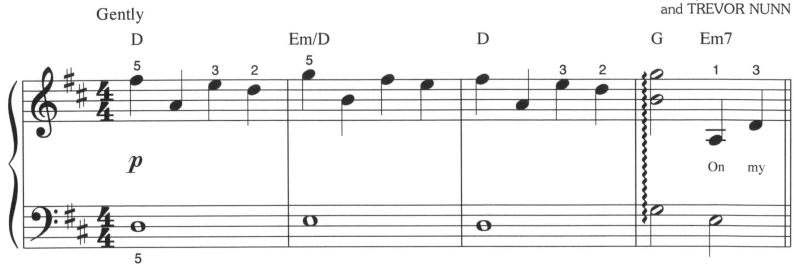

On my

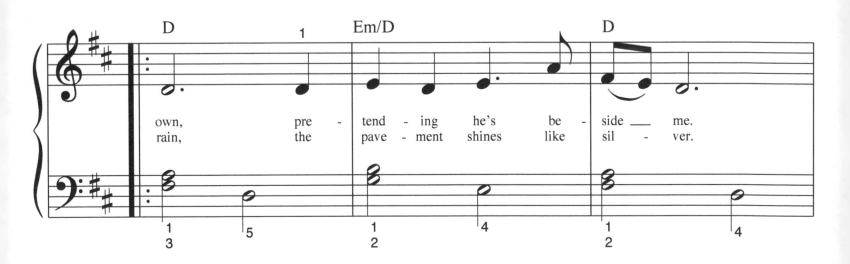

own, pre- tend- ing he's be- side ___ me.
rain, the pave- ment shines like sil- ver.

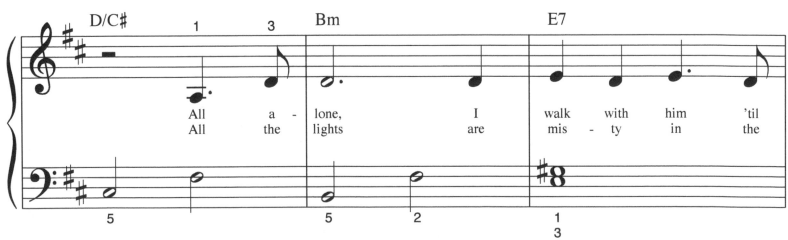

All a- lone, I walk with him 'til
All the lights are mis- ty in the

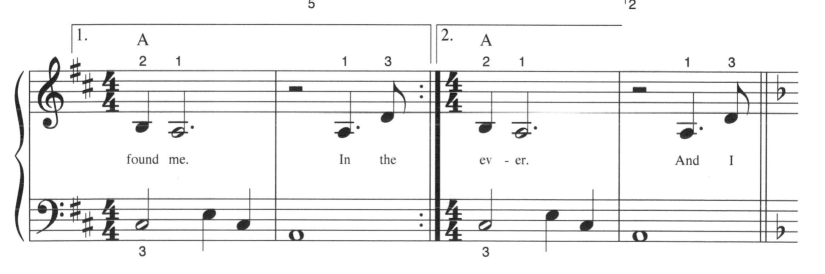

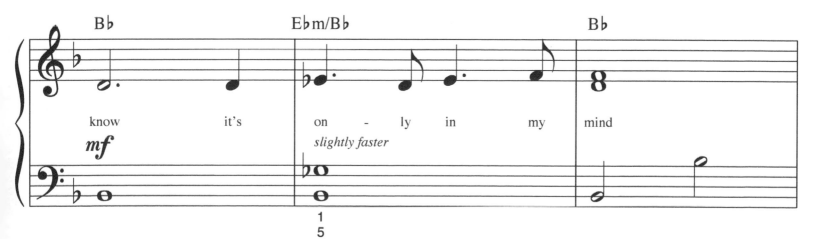

A LITTLE FALL OF RAIN

Music by CLAUDE-MICHEL SCHÖNBERG
Lyrics by ALAIN BOUBLIL, JEAN-MARC NATEL
and HERBERT KRETZMER

(EPONINE:) Don't you fret, M'sieur Mar - ius, I
don't you fret, M'sieur Mar - ius, I

don't feel an - y pain. A lit - tle fall of
don't feel an - y pain. A lit - tle fall of

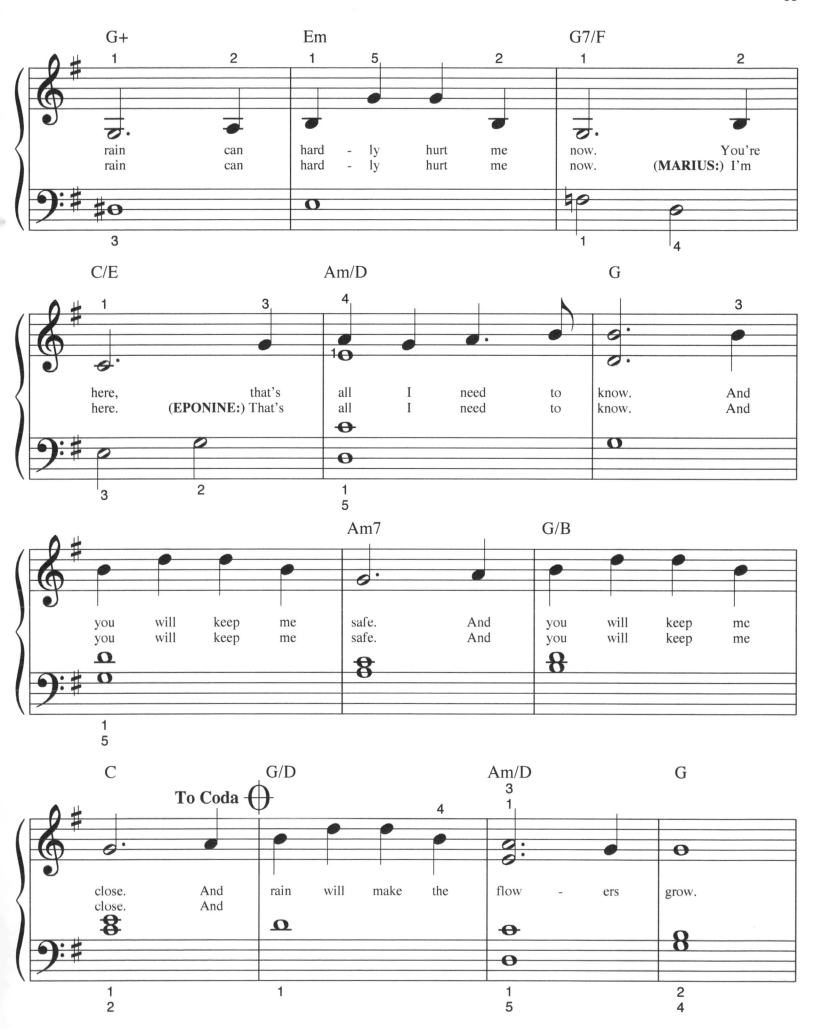

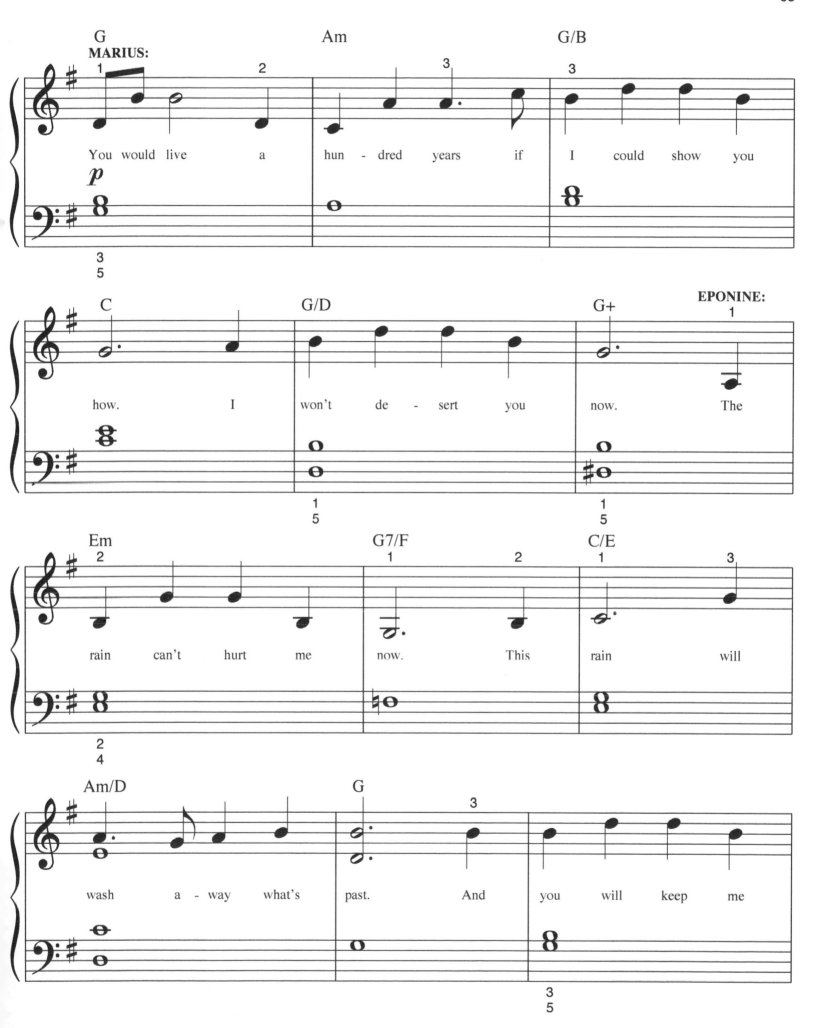

DRINK WITH ME
(TO DAYS GONE BY)

Music by CLAUDE-MICHEL SCHÖNBERG
Lyrics by ALAIN BOUBLIL and HERBERT KRETZMER

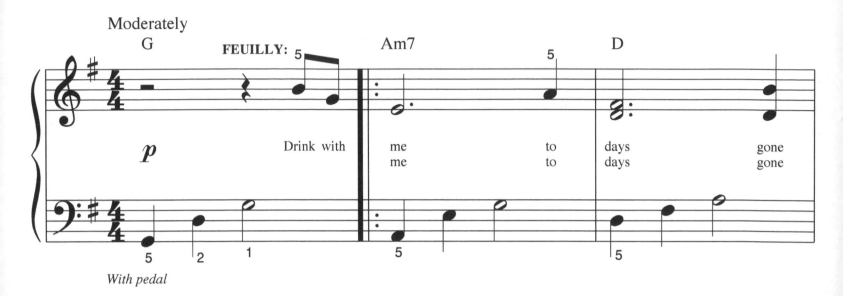

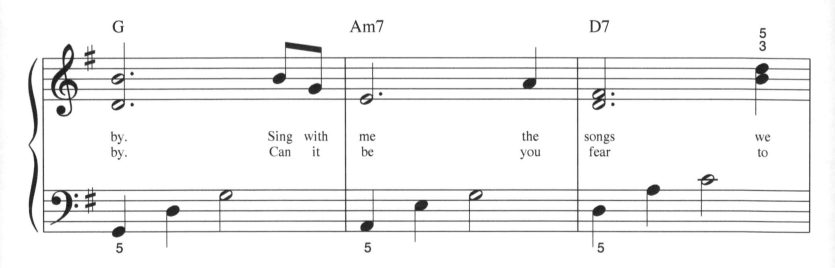

EMPTY CHAIRS AT EMPTY TABLES

Music by CLAUDE-MICHEL SCHÖNBERG
Lyrics by ALAIN BOUBLIL and HERBERT KRETZMER

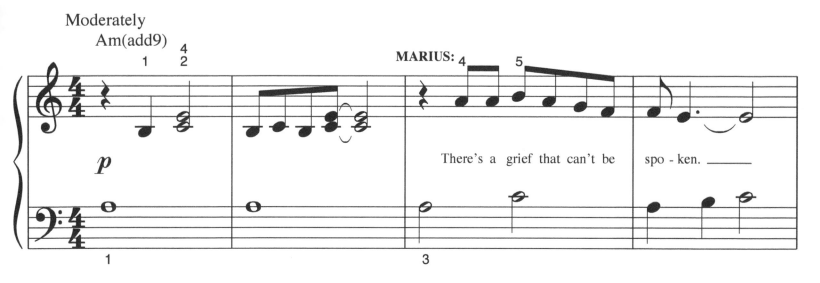

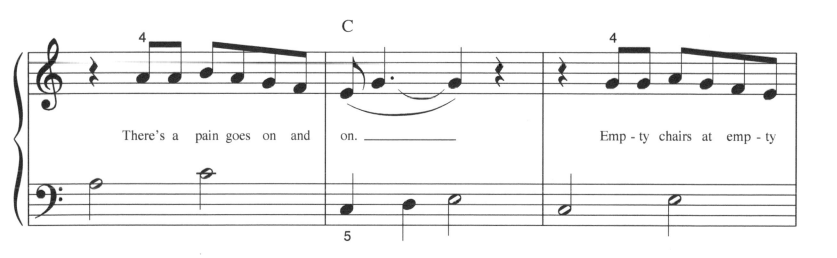

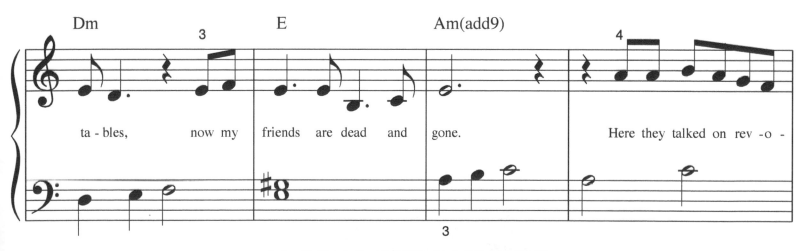

BRING HIM HOME

Music by CLAUDE-MICHEL SCHÖNBERG
Lyrics by HERBERT KRETZMER and ALAIN BOUBLIL